MW00697846

Gentle My Heart

Gentle My Heart

haiku

Nancy Rebecca Palmer

Compass Flower Press
Columbia, Missouri

Published by
Compass Flower Press
Columbia, Missouri

Library of Congress Control Number: 2023923987
ISBN: 978-1-951960-57-5

Dedicated to some who inspired me:

To my mother:

> *Years ago my mom*
> *planted a seed called writing*
> *haiku has spilled forth*

To my husband, Jack:

> *Heavenly husband*
> *who always encouraged me*
> *here is my Haiku*

To my friend, Maggie:

> *Maggie my dear friend*
> *taught me the way of haiku*
> *a wonderful gift*

Orange globe in sky
peeking over the treetops
rise to meet the day

Angel wings in clouds
a protective canopy
bringing calm and peace

The sound of nature
birdies chirping, frogs croaking
brickets add their buzz

I will sit with you
during the dark time that is
until you can stand

To stand in your strength
unafraid, hopeful and calm
ready to go on

Gentle incense swirls
drifting, wispy, quietly
adorning the space

Pencils multiply
on art table one, two, three
hoping I will write

The leaves are trembling
Sun is shining through branches
lazy summer day

Full moon and fireflies
a magical way to pass
into slumberland

The noise of the world
I turn it off and come home
to my heart being

Dancing the crescent
creativity flowing
throughout the portals

The divine moon shines
upon my weary, sad heart
a solace for now

Daily mysteries
into the unknown I go
hoping and praying

Diamonds on branches
twinkling from lovely spring rain
bringing refreshment

Memories arise
and echo gently through time
bringing me to now

A deer and full moon
this is how my day begins
truly amazing

TV tentacles
strong invisible magnets
luring souls away

Reach for ideas
Inspiration is present
will help you create

Who sent the song birds
to lift my soul from despair
gratitude for gift

The mothership cloud
silently glides overhead
bringing hope and peace

Into the painting
my paintbrush seems to take me
wild creative realms

Listening to news
praying for those on front lines
many souls to lift

Honor to lives lost
let my weeping be a prayer
we will not forget

I will not listen
to emperor without clothes
he is not truthful

Looking out window
big bright beautiful full moon
bringing peaceful calm

When we lose our breath
this can be very scary
help us Great Spirit

Being in nature
is refreshing to my soul
helping me face now

Global family
risking death behind the mask
help us learn from this

Together we stand
against the horrid virus
How long will this last?

Warbling bird inspires
to keep going in lockdown
soon it will be done

We are all guilty
not having enough respect
for each other's lives

Peace came quietly
it began with a haiku
a heart opening

What will it be like
when we come out of lockdown?
Keep my heart tender

Birch tree rises up
branches touching the blue sky
quiet dignity

Five birch trees guarding
me from the great blue beyond
Spaciousness waiting

Birds chirping sweetly
hard to believe pandemic
is still happening

Covid wrecking ball
too many wonderful lives
gross devastation

Each step a prayer
for the souls that are dying
each day with covid

Not just a number
represents souls, dreams and goals
daily lives ruined

Helpless I feel now
does anyone care for this?
dreadful covid times

A restless spirit
as I watch the news reports
covid still prevails

TV reporters
talk from home environments
see lots of bookshelves!

Unbelievable
lack of leader, coverups
death, disease, and lies

Total disruption
food lines, lost jobs, homelessness
illness, death, sadness

Graduation class
Oprah says they're chosen ones
many dreams and goals

Imagine new life
new ways, new thoughts new prayers
for a bright future

My haiku writings
inspired by friend Maggie Mae
therapy for me.

Crowds are protesting
all across America
will covid spread more?

Dark moment in time
incredible sadness reigns
no justice, no peace

TV light from box
mesmerizes and distracts
from my true, best self

Unfortunately
covid still exists in world
please go away now!

Pockets of unrest
a global movement for change
listen to the cries

Breathing in beauty
bringing delight to my soul
flowers and friendship

Pressed to ground by knee
arrogant, evil, hateful
beautiful life gone

Celebrate purple
and beautiful crown chakra
walk in royalty

Thirty seven states
pandemic is now spiking
wearing masks a must!

Image folder found
a true collager's delight
scissors, glue in hand

Reporters in frames
backdrops of art, flowers, books
this is covid way

Off goes the TV
frightening images shown
too much for my soul

Butterfly kisses
we cannot do at this time
covid six-foot rule

Equanimity
is what I am striving for
during pandemic

Lesson of covid
the fragility of life
appreciate life!

Dear puppies playing
help me to forget covid
just for a moment

Violin music
lifts anxiety away
coming to calmness

Under the full moon
I feel calm and quiet peace
beautiful respite.

Internal wisdom
shows me the way to nourish
my body and mind.

The wandering mind
leads to imagination
break from covid thoughts

In autopilot
little surprises come forth
to bless and inspire

My life becomes lists
endless things to do each day
during covid time.

White pearl high in sky
ethereal clouds float by
unexpected sight

Silence of the trees
dignity, strength and pure calm
in quiet power

Beware of the screen
it is a real life sucker
depletes the spirit

Troubles of the World
are weighing me down greatly
where can I find peace?

Lunch in the garden
koi, statues, many flowers
restoring my soul

Candles are burning
with fervent prayers rising
for November third!

Protective blanket
the quiet sky above me
bringing blessed peace.

The rustle of leaves
birdies in the burning bush
sound of fluttering.

The cry of your soul
quietly people respond
strong community.

In the world of Zoom
little boxes in a row
hoping to connect.

The trees are swaying
the wind coming and going
a dance in the sky.

Into the painting
I go to be and create
a different realm.

A walk with the moon
in full anticipation
this election day!

A walk with the stars
lighting my way in the dark
giving hope and peace.

Surrounded by stars
up so high in the dark sky
quietly twinkling.

The barren branches
are budding new, lime green leaves
signals from nature.

A pile of papers
written haiku in a stack
soul encouragements.

Enter the stillness
before the cluttering starts
best way to start day.

Adjust attitude
my mind gently cajoles me
long covid winter.

The dark moonless sky
makes me ponder where you are
Is this hide and seek?

Without a haiku
what would you do to survive
laugh, jump, play inside.

What a difference
the shining moon means to me
a welcome presence.

Following the star
carrying gold, incense, myrrh
visit with the Child

Junk mail is stacked high
represents beautiful trees
a discarded waste.

Flooded with bad news
a great burden for my soul.
Running to quiet.

Listen to birdsong
calming a frazzled spirit
in the moment peace.

My worries enhance
invisible enemy
slaying the people.

Canopy of stars
twinkling ornaments up high
a silent witness

Green grass coming up
through cracks in the rough pavement
ahh tenacity.

The black screen is still
no images coming out
to disturb my soul.

Weeping willow tree
and mourning doves share sadness
of all covid deaths.

She held onto her
verse scribbled on red paper
holding onto faith.

I guess we are all
in races from birth to death
different paces.

The rich tapestry
woven with Joy, Love, Peace, Calm
a protective cloak.

Bringing me to calm
inside mandala circle
in a gentle way.

Snake in the garden
please slither away quickly
and do me no harm.

TV god is on
spewing negativity
too hard on the nerves

Ah look at you girl
being in a pandemic
has helped you blossom

Synchronicity
is happening to me now
a special moment

In the Watsu pool
aches, worries dissolve away
deep relaxation

Colors surround me
turquoise, purple and yellow
in the Watsu womb

Birthing a haiku
brings much joy and contentment
Try it and enjoy!

Delta variant
very dangerous virus
please get your vaccine!

Heaven touches Earth
to bring the dear saint back home
angel wings flutter.

Sitting by the urn
ashes of my dear husband
thankful for his life.

Soothe my soul oh Lord
feed my soul into the depths
where peace will abide.

Death a life event
going to the final edge
and flying away.

Alone in the house
listening to the quiet
sadness over loss.

Tears hiding in chest
wanting to be released soon
overflow of grief.

In expectation
my heart waits to hear from you
what joy that will bring.

The grief is deep blue
overtaking my being
and bringing me low.

Trying to survive
but I want to thrive and grow
unwavering soul.

Rest in the shadow
where it is calm and peaceful
nestled into God.

Thumping of the tail
means to me you are close by
bringing joy and awe.

Stars and wispy clouds
like a comforting blanket
over my being.

Spirit self flying
high above the clouds and earth
looking down in awe.

Fierce rainbows glisten
pulsating golden goblet
trees rejoice in wind.

Waiting for a sign
coming only from my love
struggle for patience.

Puppies at my side
so devoted and loving
keeping me going.

Chair full of Santas
in honor and memory
of holiday joy.

Help me find a way
to bridge the gap between us
I am here for you.

Invisible threads
pulling gently my heart strings
moving me forward.

I prepare a place
that we can meet together
with meditation.

A dose of the moon
Big, beautiful Moon up high
glowing down on me.

Portal within me
taking me to realms unknown
kingdom of most High.

Walking with the moon
in the cold winter weather
waking me to now!

Please quiet my soul
let me rest in your presence
to deep calm and peace.

Angels unaware
are you right there before me
please protect my soul

Candles burn brightly
illuminating calmness
to my troubled soul.

The sound of sirens
inspiring puppy to howl
like urgent prayers.

Snowy trees swaying
gently back and forth they move
whispering there, there.

Raise my vibrations
into the heavenly realms
to dance among stars

Early morning walks
are very good for the soul
thankful for puppies.

Depression lurks close
bills piling up day by day—
be gone foul illness.

True God, living God
breathe your holy breath on me
to bring me closer.

Snow flurry dances
while stirring the energy
creating magic.

My right hand holds on
so thankful for your right hand
to give me safety.

And just like that you
were lifted up and away
to faraway realms

I have to breathe now
so I can enter this space
with all my being

Preparing for flight
I let it all fade away
so I can soar high.

Reaching to Heaven
to get a touch from my love
rour presence close by.

Swaying trees are back
bringing solace and peace to
my anxious sad soul.

Images of war
overwhelm the tender soul
where can we find peace?

Graciously removed
from hideous war horrors
to a place of calm.

Stop the ugly war
please stop the cruelty now
bring peace and healing.

The love of my life
communicated to me
through a medium.

From the other side
words of comfort come to me
bringing joy and peace.

Body tossed in ditch
unceremoniously
with no funeral.

Circle energy
The sound of drums, wind blowing
creating magic.

Moon peeking through clouds
full, beautiful and glowing
this Easter Sunday.

Gold Finch and bright light
evidence of your presence
brings joy to my heart.

If you would come to
my inner heart chamber now
you would behold love.

The light that calls me
reminds me that you are near
I love you dearly.

Spirit man show up
for me and we will dance now
together in joy.

Emmanuel and
angels helping with comfort
a sweet protection.

Corner light shining
it is your gentle touch and
your quiet presence.

Big, bright beautiful
as if to say *look at me!*
After the eclipse.

Looking into Blue
high above my head the sky
fingernail moon peeks.

Congo line moving
Cuban music fills the air
dancing the circle.

Standing out in crowd
the lavender kimono
on lady of joy.

Saturate my soul
with loving kindness for all
for the collective.

Indigo bunting
and big, glorious full moon
two simple pleasures.

Within the circle
is safety, a boundary
life-giving to me.

Possibilities
abound if we open hearts
and minds to believe.

Your death opens me
to discover my own truth
for my highest good.

Working in silence
you know, the deep depths of soul
where portals emerge.

Across time and space
will I find you again soon?
The cry of my heart.

Tornado inside
it must swirl out to release
emotions so deep.

Napping puppies at
my feet and under star quilt
bringing much comfort.

Inside garden thrives
green leaves stretching and growing
pink orchid stands tall.

Lots of whys spinning
and twirling over my head
causing me to weep.

When and while I can
to walk in a way pleasing
to the most high God.

Seeking the shadow
where all is calm and peaceful
resting in safety.

Old man and black dog
every morning walking slow
such dedication.

Vibrational flow
back and forth, pinging and pong
coming to stillness.

Nourish your being
breathe, practice gentle kindness
come into worship.

The different views
the clearing takes patient time
then peace will begin.

Fingernail moon shines
against the darkest blue sky
a sweet calm sighting.

A bench in the cold
surrounded by snowy trees
feeling all alone.

Childlike wonder sweeps
across the old lady's face
bringing youthful joy.

Moonless sky above
how I miss your shiny face
make a swift return!

What a blow your death
to the very depths of soul
leaving me broken.

Ring of a good man
now on my middle finger
memory of you.

Yellow butterfly
is that you my sweet darling?
How long do I wait?

Cessna high in sky
causing curiosity—
are you passing by?

Wind in trees, leaves fall
colors changing, crispy air—
Oh how I love Fall!

Yellow butterflies
Cessna high in the sky, lights
blinking signs of you.

The persimmon tree
release your fruit for me please
so pudding is made.

By myself again
life unfolding, quietly
not as expected.

By myself with God
and Lady Guadalupe
angel guardian

The dry crackly leaves
tumbling across the concrete
like a death rattle.

Waiting for the rain
wind blowing, puppy howling
anticipation.

Once upon a moon
I had a handsome husband
now he is Spirit.

Gray skies, barren trees
winter cold settling in now
wanting inward life.

Silence uncovers
a deep ache in my being
wanting to be soothed.

Hibiscus angels
keeping watch over my life
bringing peace and calm.

Blood moon and the stars
a celestial delight
majestic splendor.

Red moon hovering
high in the early morning
over sleepy town.

Beloved goldens
on either side of me now
bringing such comfort.

Husband in Heaven
how are you today my dear?
sending you sweet hugs.

Stirring in the house
folks waking up to new day
what is in store next?

Arising from heart
bubbling up to the surface
feelings from past times

Looking out window
white dog, sunlight, pine branches
framed by lace curtains.

Gazing out window
bird flying by, high in sky
free, without a care.

Waiting on the earth
until my departure time
to see husband's face.

to see my husband
again would be so joyful
to my deepest soul.

Stuffed unicorns strewn
all across my bedroom floor
sign of puppy play.

Puppy gathering
on top of the old star quilt
cozy and comfy.

All things wonderful
bright full moon, crispy fall day
golden retrievers.

Leaning in to hear
the whisper of the Divine
gentle and calming.

Christmas cactus blooms
bringing a delightful joy
and pure happiness.

Paper filled boxes
these old hat boxes on shelf
lots of history

The dancing green lights
aurora borealis
so mesmerizing.

Leaves bouncing on road
like confetti so happy
playful and joyful.

Deserted building
oh the stories it could tell
now so desolate.

Silence of the urn
I observe in sacred space
the great mystery.

I don't want to show
you my broken pieces deep
within my sad heart.

They are hidden there
and make me so sad to view
and realize truth.

Pink clouded sunrise
like a soft water color
a divine painting.

Blinking Christmas lights
around blow up figures Grinch,
Snowman and Santa.

Seems sort of tacky
but in a strange way so fun
bringing some whimsy.

I can see into
the great vastness inside me
the Kingdom of God.

Big, old, red bible
a favorite possession
to have very near.

When I get my wings
I will fly so high and smooth
over many lands.

Hibiscus blooms full
and the big beautiful moon
two gifts for the day.

Walking with the moon
glowing, white orb high above
good energy flows

A leaf gently falls
silently to the soft grass
from the old oak tree.

Five deer and full moon
simple pleasures to enjoy
in the early morn.

Loose ends here and there
soul desires a completion
to several things.

Now is the moment
not the past or the future
now is energy.

Cardinal high up
singing and swaying on branch
seems safe and happy.

Walking in silence
pondering great mysteries
with no conclusion.

Sound bath vibrations
causing shifts in my being
moving out the old

Refreshing my soul
creating space for new thoughts
ideas and dreams.

I have heard silence
with a faint bit of birdsong
quieting my soul.

Wood circle maker
mandala maker also
colorful delight.

Edgy feelings fly
through the air polluting space
not good start to day.

The departure signs
praying angel with flowers
birdsong and sunlight.

Under crescent moon
I hear such lovely tunes
lifting the soul high.

The clouds are silent
but communicate so much
peace, calm, gentleness.

American Flag
Flying half-mast once again
reason: school shooting.

over and over
many, many senseless deaths
because of hard hearts

Lawmaker what if
this was one of your children
would there be a change?

A bit of whimsy
is something everyone wants
here and there in life.

Sunning on back deck
breezes, wind and sweet birdsong
a delightful day.

The tree blocks the sun
creating beautiful shade
A nature blessing.

Conversation piece
transformation of table
into funky art.

Coming to the mat
at beloved yoga class
stretching and breathing.

So many lessons
with mind, body and spirit
always in my heart.

rest deeply and breath
on mat lying flat on back
Spirit rising free.

Your death was a blow
to the heart of my being
everything did change.

Magazine perfect
the photos all in a row
could it be airbrush?

Thoughts like clouds gliding
across the vast azure sky
coming and going.

Wind chimes and sweet sounds
tinkling in soft gentle winds
bringing needed joy.

Out of box thinker
that is what I am doing
finding fun places.

Moon covered by clouds
creating an eerie glow
Bringing mystery.

Candle burning bright
full moon shining from above
Into the quiet.

Like a butterfly
precisely a yellow one
he comes to visit.

Pinkish glow to moon
soothing to the depths of soul
all is well... it is.

Truth and honesty
for the good of the people
brings needed comfort.

Haikus keep coming
ideas tumble around
until written down.

They make fun of me
for going to bed early
I will have last laugh.

The celestial realm
gloriously high above
within unseen world

At your feet I sit
soaking up your love and light
so I will be strong.

Sunlight is beaming
nature outside my window
lots of greenery.

Birdsong is galore
cardinals flying circles
nature so alive.

Early morning hour
such a sweetness that dwells here
in blessed quiet.

Candles burning bright
to bring light to my dark soul
helping me survive.

Flung out of structure
feeling like flying out there
amongst trees and space.

Acknowledgment

This collection of haiku is a result of encouragement from my dear friend, Maggie Megalynn, who introduced me to this form of poetry. I found haiku a way to express myself.

As I played with haiku, it became an important part of my self-care through covid, the death of my husband, war in Ukraine, a daughter Jennifer enduring a six-month illness, and more.

Reading through these poems, I realized what a balm to my soul nature is. Also, I noted that during times of stress and grief I tend to look up, thus, my haiku verse included the moon, stars, sun, clouds, and trees.

This book is my way to honor the truth that came forth.

Acknowledgment

Peace came quietly
it began with a haiku
a heart opening.

Birthing a haiku
brings much joy and contentment
try it and enjoy

—nrp